ONCE UPON A TIME

The Stories of a Loyal House

R. C. Westland

TotalRecall Publications, Inc..
1103 Middlecreek
Friendswood, Texas 77546
281-992-3131
www.totalrecallpress.com

All rights reserved. Except as permitted under the United States Copyright Act of 1976. no part of this publication may be reproduced, stored in a retrieval system, or transmitted in any form or by any means electronic or mechanical or by photocopying, recording, or otherwise without prior permission of the publisher. Exclusive worldwide content publication / distribution by TotalRecall Publications, Inc..

Copyright © 2022 by: R. C. Westland
Copyright Cover © by: Oil-on-board, H. Richmond
All rights reserved

ISBN: 978-1-64883-148-5
UPC: 6-43977-41485-4
FIRST EDITION
1 2 3 4 5 6 7 8 9 10

Library of Congress Control Number: 2022933671

An Historical Non-Fiction Novel
The stories about the house at #113 Montague Street are true and based on facts researched by the author.

The scanning, uploading and distribution of this book via the Internet or via any other means without the permission of the publisher is illegal and punishable by law. Please purchase only authorized electronic editions, and do not participate in or encourage electronic piracy of copyrighted materials. Your support of the author's rights is appreciated.

These stories are dedicated to the staff and volunteers of the Charlotte County Archives and the St. Andrews Civic Trust.

Without their ongoing commitment to history and architecture, books like this one could not be written.

ABOUT THE AUTHOR

Rem Westland is the author of numerous short stories, a non-fiction account of his run for political office in a federal election, and two novels. After a career spent mostly in Canada's capital city, the sea-side town of St. Andrews beckoned. The town became the setting for his second novel, and for these stories.

ACKNOWLEDGEMENTS

A special "thank-you" to Emily Somers, an artist based in St. Stephen, New Brunswick, who sketched the original images that appear in this publication. St. Stephen is the next town over from St. Andrews, closer by water than by road.

Michelle Roy, of St. Croix Printing & Publishing Co Ltd, was always available to present the manuscript in "final" form at its various stages of development. The river St. Croix has marked the boundary between Canada and the United States of America since 1783.

Copy edit support was provided by Sigrid Macdonald (Book Magic Inc, Florida). The advice of professional editor Maeve O'Connell (Toronto), on content, was invaluable. Also invaluable was research done by Marie La Forest. Her many photographs are attributed to MLF in the text.

Bruce Moran, of Total Recall Publications Inc, was on stand-by from the start. To know TRP would help bring these stories to the reading public kept the production team going.

Motivation to tell these stories came from the house itself. If you are in St. Andrews some day, take a walk past the place. What you see is what loyalty looks like.

The stories of this house adhere to the facts. If the logic which supports the leap from one fact to another is deficient, responsibility for the deficiency lies entirely with the author.

FOREWORD

The house at #113 Montague Street, St. Andrews, New Brunswick, Canada sits on a lot assigned in 1784 to a United Empire Loyalist. The Loyalists, numbering between forty and fifty thousand, were British citizens residing in the New England colonies who stayed true to King George III during the American Revolution. The Loyalists fled America in fear for their lives. In France, a strong ally of the emerging republic, tens of thousands of citizens who stayed loyal to their king were executed.

For a built structure on the north-east coast of North America, #113 is very old.

Fieldstone, deposited during the earth's last glacial period, was used for the foundation. The trunks of centuries-old cedar trees – axed and sawn by hand – supported joists hewn from oaks. The oaks were a hundred years older than the cedars. Studs for the walls, and planks for the floors and roof, came from lumber mills established alongside tributaries of the Penobscot River well before Maine became the twenty-third state of the United States of America. The first windows were cut from glass fired in England at pre-industrial age foundries.

If the mix of minerals, fibres, chemicals, and water that are the substance of a house also brings awareness, if walls had ears, #113 would have overheard when the residents inside – one generation of owners after another – spoke about George Washington, Napoleon, Catherine the Great, John A. Macdonald, Vladimir Lenin, Adolph Hitler, Mao Zedong, John Diefenbaker, Pierre and then Justin Trudeau. If clapboard on the outside could see, this house would have watched as soldiers marched down Montague Street in 1814 and ambled by on furlough during two world wars.

The roof of this house held on tightly when a tropical cyclone blew dozens of other places in St. Andrews apart. The Saxby Gale, in 1869, did not get through the oak front door.

Behind that oak front door there is a large room on each side of a tiny foyer. A narrow stairway rises steeply to two rooms on the second floor. The upstairs rooms have sloped ceilings that rise at the same angle as the stairs. They are divided by a water-closet (sink and toilet).

Off the downstairs room on the right is a well-appointed kitchen that shares the width of the house with a full bathroom. The kitchen opens to a family room. As many as six adults can sit comfortably in that airy, fifteen-foot square, room for an evening of lively discussion. The visitors among them would have entered through the back door – never, in the Maritimes, through the front.

A long hallway runs from the back door. At the far end is a double-hung window, with nine rectangular sections. Attentive visitors would see that a bubbled glass pane, in the lower left corner of the window, is cracked. Everything else in the house is finished to perfection.

Though the undulations of clay underground have rendered every architectural line of the house off-true, the trim around windows and doors fits exactly at every joint. The walls inside have been re-plastered and the floor boards are new. Only that one little pane of glass hints at two and a half centuries of turbulence.

The first residents of this house read angry letters from relatives who stayed in the new republic. Decades later, residents tuned-in to voices from across the Atlantic when radio arrived. They talked to friends in Europe by telephone when Graham

Bell's invention was wired in. They were amazed when human voices reached earth from the moon. They communicated with strangers across the globe when the internet took over.

Through all those years, this house stayed silent.

What follows are stories this house has waited a very long time to tell. The stories are a salute, and a thank-you, to the people who built it, repaired it, and improved upon it, with the thought that #113 might be around forever.

TABLE OF CONTENTS

About The Author iv

Acknowledgements v

Foreword vi

Part 1: Heartbreak And War 1

Part 2: A Place Of Refuge 14

Part 3: Early Transfers 24

Part 4: Perseverance Through Change 43

Part 5: Hop Scotch 56

Afterword 70

Inventory Of Sources 75

PART 1:
HEARTBREAK AND WAR

On a cadastral map of St. Andrews, drawn in 1784, there are eight lots in block F. The name written into the space for lot #7 is John Crafford.

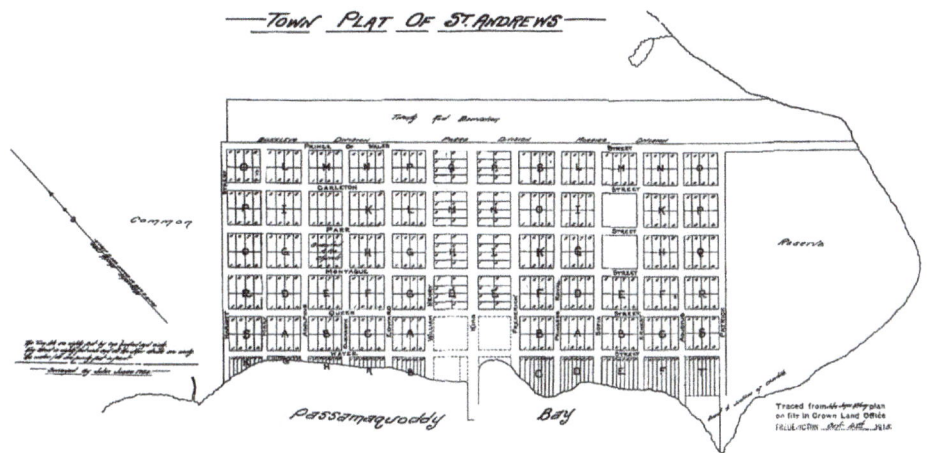

Credit to Charlotte County Archives.

John Crafford's life on the Atlantic coast, however, began thirty years earlier.

The Scottish Jacobite army was slaughtered in the 1746 Battle of Culloden, close to where the Crafford family lived. The "Butcher" of Culloden, the English Duke of Cumberland, then had his troops roam the countryside to hunt down and kill surviving sympathisers of the Scottish cause – the restoration of a Stuart king to the British throne. A forced transfer of land from Scottish farmers to English aristocracy would soon follow. It would bring years of great starvation to the clans.

All across the Highlands, the collapse of family farms saw young men be sent away by their fathers and mothers. They were sent to be apprenticed for the trades in Glasgow and Edinburgh. They were sent to uncertain futures in North America. In the late summer of 1753, a "John Crawford" had passage on the brig *Dolphin* that sailed from Greenock, Scotland to the New World. He was probably in his teens.

There are a half-dozen ways to approximate the spelling of John Crafford's name. It comes from "crawa" – meaning "crow" – and "ford" – where a stream can be crossed. The earliest Craffords, when names were assigned for administrative reasons, lived on the hillsides, near running water, where crows were a common presence.

Credit to Emily Somers.

A Thomas Crawfurd, probably related, had been ennobled and granted land within the city limits of Greenock by King James II in 1669. *Crawfurd's Dyke* was the name given to a long quay running into the sea from the shore along his property. In the 1750s thousands of émigrés departed every year from the quay that still carried the Crawfurd name. By then, Crawfurd's mansion was a ruin. Greenock's town core had become a rotting slum.

Brigs like the *Dolphin*, a twenty-four-gun navy frigate with square-rigged masts, were popular in their day. They were relatively fast, maneuverable, and versatile. The *Dolphin* is recorded to have carried passengers in the 1750s, was devoted to survey work in the 1760s, and was committed to warfare during the military phase of the American Revolution.

In 1753, under the command of Captain Cooters, the *Dolphin*'s destination was Bagaduce, a place-name derived from the Mi'kmaq word for the Penobscot Bay area now in the state of Maine. The voyage from Greenock to Bagaduce could take as long as five weeks on the roiling seas.

There were some sixty adults and a dozen children on the ship. The men and older boys had been recruited by *Waldo* corporation, a family-owned head-hunter that provided workers to the British military for infrastructure development in New England. Included among them was Ebenezer Greenlaw, a youth sixteen years of age who travelled with three brothers. Like John Crafford, the Greenlaws did not expect to ever see their parents again.

Credit to Gordon Johnson, Pixabay.

✭✭✭✭✭

Crafford, Greenlaw, Greenlaw's brothers, other men and older boys on board the *Dolphin* had signed four-year contracts to work off the cost of their voyage. Crafford's occupation was listed as *herdsman*, making him one of few on board who were not tradesmen (mechanic, weaver, brewer, book binder). Most of the passengers came from the same area in the Scottish Highlands. Many likely knew one another before embarkation.

The travellers worried about the "wild beasts" and "Indian" hostilities they might encounter in the New World. The image of wild beasts was exacerbated by fairy tales. The fear of Indians, on the other hand, was drawn from newspaper reports. The tension between settlers on the Atlantic coast of America and Indigenous peoples – attributed by historians to the Treaty of Utrecht (1713-1715) because it legitimized land grabs by European powers – was very real. Flare-ups were frequent.

The flare-ups were enthusiastically reported in all their ghastly detail in the newspapers of Scotland in John Crafford's day. In Edinburgh's *General Evening Post* of July 18, 1751, the scalping of a woman in New England was described and the fate of twenty men and women taken captive in the same raid was speculated upon. Reporters often used the words *Indian Wars*. Readers were spared none of the gory details.

In New England the Greenock-boarded passengers would be settling upriver on the Penobscot, at a place two miles from the sea. This gave comfort. Rivers and coasts provided mobility in an era of thick woods and no roads. Gun boats could patrol the shore. Sea coasts and rivers provided fish for food.

The passengers were told there would be accommodations waiting for them in America upon arrival. In this regard, they were disappointed. *Waldo* had begun construction on a large common house for all married men with families to live in, but the roof was never built. The half-built structure was allowed to deteriorate rather than be completed. Single men built military-style huts – dug into the ground, with straw roofs and blanket-dividers on the inside. Families were temporarily distributed among the houses of settlers already living there.

Credit to Emily Somers.

The homes the newcomers would build over the next four years reflected the style of "folk house" that they had left behind. It was a style that, in New England, would become known as *Cape Cod*.

The American Revolution – a political, then ideological, then military event – began in 1765, twelve years after the *Dolphin* deposited John Crafford and the Greenlaw brothers ashore. After their first four years with *Waldo*, likely lumbering wood for ship repair and trade, they had eighteen years to settle in before the tension in America became active warfare. John Crafford had at least three dependents by then, probably a wife and two children.

Midway through the military phase of the American Revolution, in 1779, the British military conscripted workers to build Fort George near the site of a former French fortification. Fort Pentagouet had been built by France in the 1630s to protect trade routes. The French fort was temporarily Dutch in 1674 and again in 1676. A hundred years later, it was a mound of earth.

Fort George was built to be part of a defence line aimed to keep American revolutionary forces south of the Penobscot River. Military leaders expected to lose the war. They expected the Penobscot to become the border between British North America and the thirteen colonies of New England. The name *New Ireland* had been picked for the British colony that the Penobscot area would have become. A few years later the name would be floated again for what became the province of New Brunswick, in Canada.

By 1783 the American Revolution had driven thousands of loyal colonists from as far south as Boston to the safe area around Fort George. The fighting had been fierce.

For a myriad of reasons, one of which was love for the Crown and another was distrust of disorder, the colonists who fled north were people who wanted to remain British. Perhaps the most compelling reason for some was that the British administration had become an important source of revenue as an employer or as a procurer of goods and services.

When the American Revolution finally ended, residents in the Fort George area – whether long term or recently relocated for safety – expected to remain British. Those loyal to the Crown were betrayed. Even though that part of Maine – a region within the jurisdiction of Massachusetts until 1820 – had remained solidly in British hands and Fort George never fell, peace negotiators in Europe agreed to America's insistence that the border be set farther north.

Credit to the Tides Institute & Museum of Art, Eastport, Maine.

British government leaders acceded to American demands because their priority was the threat of war in Europe. France, England's likely enemy, was already America's greatest friend. In the thirteen colonies that became the United States, French national emblems like the eagle were raised high. In Castine, the French national flower – the *fleur de lis* – was integral to many of the crests in town and remains so today.

Credit to Castine Historical Society, Castine, Maine.

The boundary would therefore begin where the Americans – Benjamin Franklin and John Adams among them – said it should: at the mouth of the St. Croix River, and run from there to the highlands of the interior. It would take a few months before the Americans and the British could agree where the mouth of the St. Croix actually was. It would take fifty years and the "Aroostook War" for the British and American governments to agree upon the geographical location of the highlands. Two hundred and forty years later the ownership of Mathias Seal Island off the New England coast would still be in dispute.

✯✯✯✯✯

While negotiations that would establish the boundary between the victorious United States and British North America were underway, colonists who wanted to remain British had an increasingly hard life. The pejorative word *Tory*, drawn from the politics of the day to denote opposition to change, was shouted at them in public places. They were physically abused on the streets and in their homes.

The house of Benjamin Milliken, a wealthy lumber mill owner in Scarborough (now in Maine) was plundered, his cattle slaughtered, and a maid had three fingers slashed by the sword of a republican when she tried to lock up the silver. Milliken's maid was reported to have pointed at her fingers and shouted at her assailant: *There, sir, is better blood than ever runs in your veins.* The next swipe of the sword took off her hand.

Credit to Emily Somers.

Ebenezer Greenlaw wrote *A True Account of My Sufferings*. He described the loss of his home, his barn, his animals, and all other assets when the rebels prevailed. He was tortured by being lifted by a rope around his neck and made to stand on tip-toe to avoid strangulation. He remained in irons for an extensive period. Just prior to release, he was threatened by bayonet. Records archived in Castine say that Ebenezer died. Though four in his and Crafford's group were executed by knife, Ebenezer Greenlaw actually managed to escape.

There were dozens of stories like those of Milliken and Greenlaw. The military commander of American forces in the Penobscot area warned those who had stayed loyal to Britain: **Get out, or else!**

Sir Guy Carleton, commander-in-chief of the British forces, took the warning seriously. He received permission from London to move loyal colony residents to safe havens in Nova Scotia and in what would become New Brunswick. For those who wanted to leave, it was time to get organized.

John Crafford, Ebenezer Greenlaw, and two of his three brothers signed up with a Castine-based organization that called itself the Penobscot Association. There were 643 men, women, and children on the list.

Once organized, the next step for the Association was to decide where to go. After a tour by its leaders of alternative sites north of the St. Croix, the Association chose St. Andrews, in soon-to-be named Charlotte County, on the shore of the Passamaquoddy Bay. The lay of the land was similar to that around Castine. The weather was comparable. Robert Pagan, one of the leaders on the tour, wrote about thousands of acres of standing hardwood and a great location from which to launch trade with the British West Indies.

★★★★★

The fleet of British vessels which carried the Association to St. Andrews included their goods and animals, and some 200 British soldiers. A half-dozen barges were loaded with timber, shingles, windows, and hardware taken from dismantled Castine houses and public buildings. It was October, 1783.

Given how cumbersome construction was in those days (felling of trees, hewing of wood into beams and boards by axe, carving wooden pegs), plus the scarcity of iron nails, hinges, and other hardware, it made sense for the British to take standing infrastructure apart and ship with them as much of the material as possible. There was no sympathy for the rebel Americans who were dispossessed.

Spare a thought, however, for the republicans who stayed. Their dispossession must have been traumatic. When serving bacon and eggs to a visiting St. Andrews couple in 2017, the server, a young Castine woman, observed: *you people have our houses!*

For their part, every departing member of the Penobscot Association – every man, woman, and child – left someone behind. Many adult children stayed when parents elected to go. Brothers and sisters said farewell. Boys and girls had a last hug from grandparents. Uncles and aunts who opted for the new republic might never see nieces and nephews again. Neighbours on shore waved to friends who oared away in flat-bottomed American *bateaux*. The eyes of most who watched the departures were filled with tears. The eyes of some were filled with hate.

The mass movement of United Empire Loyalists (UEL), a title the Governor-in-Chief of British North America granted them in

1789, has been described as the first organized large-scale evacuation of refugees in the modern era. More than 30,000 Loyalists fled from the newly-minted United States to Nova Scotia and New Brunswick. Over 8,000 went to Upper Canada/Ontario, and 2,000 more went to Lower Canada/Quebec.

PART 2:
A PLACE OF REFUGE

The Penobscot Association was well managed by its leaders, Robert Pagan chief among them. All on board the ships in the fleet knew what lots they would be assigned prior to embarkation. There would be no rush for land upon landing. Pagan wanted none of the anarchy that had, in his view, marked the approach of revolutionaries in America. He wanted stability.

And stability, he got. Until the mid-1900s, the length and breadth of the lot assigned to John Crafford (eighty by sixty feet) stayed just as Charles Morris, a young army lieutenant and deputy-surveyor with the British military, set out in his cadastral map. The lot fronts Montague Street. It is one property in from Edward Street and two properties over from Elizabeth Street.

Until 1865, the house on lot #7 was the only one that stood on the north-eastern half of block F. Lots number #6 and #5 on its left, and lot #8 on its right, stayed vacant for over seventy years.

The vacancy years are interesting: they should not have happened! British policy required owners to show "improvement" upon granted land within one year or have that land be re-granted. The line up of British nationals who wanted land at the turn of the eighteenth century, whether escaping America or emigrating from the British Isles, was long.

✭✭✭✭✭

Land grant #95 made the assignment to John Crafford of his town lot official. In the same land grant, lot #8 was assigned to Ebenezer Greenlaw. Benjamin Milliken, the wealthy lumber mill owner whose maid had lost her hand, was granted a double lot that backed upon Crafford's and Greenlaw's properties. Town lots were allocated to 351 other Penobscot UEL. All Association members, on a controlled basis managed by British administrators, would have access to the boards, beams, windows, shingles, hardware, tools, clothing, and livestock brought over from Castine.

Land grant #96 provided 100 acres of back-land to 188 of those same Loyalists, Greenlaw and Crafford among them. The fact that twice as many grantees received town lots confirms that St. Andrews, from the start, was a place for merchants rather than for farmers.

The merchants of St. Andrews were actively trading with American colonies and the British West Indies within their first year. Lumber, supplies for ships, and fish dominated the trade. Ship building soon followed. Town residents paid for the produce of the surrounding farms with promissory notes (common at the time) and cash (rare).

By 1783 Crafford would have learned how to adapt his skills as a herder to conditions along the Atlantic coast. He would still have been vigorous enough to make a "go" of it all over again. Until 1865, however, his was the only lot in the north-eastern half of block F to have a house built upon it. John did not develop his 100 acres of back-land, which were re-granted as per British policy in 1790. It suggests that, when others with lots on his side of block F opted to settle on their farms, John Crafford preferred to stay in town.

As a full-time resident in town, Crafford may have been welcomed by Ebenezer Greenlaw and other neighbours to "improve" their properties by felling trees and pasturing a farm animal or two. The three other lots along Montague Street were never re-granted.

Visiting British politicians, administrators, and military officers were impressed by the energy displayed by the residents of St. Andrews. The cost of sailing a fully armed frigate (*Ariadne*) up and down the coast during the first winter of 1783-1784 was deemed to be worth it. Ten years later the patrols continued. In the spring of 1795 a privateer and his sloop-of-war *Union* sailed up and down the harbour to keep away Indian "troublemakers" who would otherwise have distracted settlers from the tasks at hand.

Credit to Emily Somers.

What the Indigenous people wanted, of course, was a square deal. It was an objective pressed upon the newly-arrived colonists in 1783, and was still being pursued by the Passamaquoddy in negotiations with Canada's federal government two hundred and forty years later.

✶✶✶✶✶

British naval engineers had been harvesting tall pine on the shores of the Passamaquoddy for masts and ship-length boards since the 1760s. Now, with the arrival of the Association, there was a flourish of enthusiasm to clear away remaining scrub brush and smaller trees. It would be many years, however, before a person could walk at night in St. Andrews without fearing injury from the thousands of stumps left behind by the navy. Amid the stumps, the town was at first an unsightly mixture of tents, lean-tos, wicker cottages, and log or clapboard houses.

Credit to Emily Somers.

The look of Slabtown on the fringe of St. Andrews – shanties built from cedar "slabs" by Blacks who came north as indentured servants or were former slaves – was a whole lot worse. Slabs were strips of cedar bark, axed or sawn away from the cleaned logs that were used by everyone else.

✶✶✶✶✶

During the first few years the focus of clearance was King Street, near the centre of town, and then stretches north and south on Water Street along the coast. Construction of public buildings had priority. Warehouses, shops, and quays came next.

To build private homes, property owners petitioned for a share of the Castine supply and for support from reserve and serving military engineers. As the first French explorers – including Samuel de Champlain, first Governor of New France – learned when they overwintered on the Isle St. Croix in 1604, the weather gets very cold, very quickly, when winter comes. To dither was not an option.

Since 1790 was the year when John Crafford's back-land acres were re-granted, he likely had a house in town by then. The Castine supply was declared exhausted in that same year.

A hand-drawn map held by the Charlotte County Archives of St. Andrews dated 1844 is definitely wrong. It does not feature a standing house on the north-eastern side of block F facing Montague Street.

A hand-written letter dated 1823, also at the Charlotte County Archives, transfers lot #7 with "land, premises, and appurtenances" from an Edward Parker to his mother. Further, in 1829, Alexander Strachan is quoted in the files to say that the north-eastern half of block F is "where I now reside." More is said about Edward, his mother, and Alexander in the paragraphs below.

✶✶✶✶✶

There are a number of clues dating the construction of #113 Montague Street to 1790 or earlier. For one thing, there are handy comparisons. The house at #113 is different from what Arthur

Richmond, in his book *The Evolution of the Cape Cod House,* calls a "standard" Cape. There is one window on each side of the central door, not two. This is a style he found to be rare, and older.

The house at #113 is not a Three-Quarter Cape (one window on one side of the door, two windows on the other). Nor is it a Half-Cape (door on one side, two windows to the left or right of the door).

Credit to the Charlotte County Archives.

Number 113 is identical, however, to the "Loyalist House" that still stands in the next block over. It is also identical to the "old St. Andrews coffee house" relocated by Andrew Martin to the corner of Water and William Streets (burnt in 1930). Both those other two houses were moved in their entirety from Castine – taken down piece by piece and reconstructed. Two standard

Capes are pictured in old photographs, one to the immediate left of the Kirk on Montague and one standing opposite the Kirk on the corner of Edward Street.

A seeming clincher regarding material used for the construction of #113 is that gables in the roof of the ell are supported by trusses held in place by square-cut iron nails. Square cut nails are driven into partially hewn joists in the basement of the house as well. Nails of this kind were manufactured in the second half of the 1700s in the New England colonies.

In one of the upstairs bedrooms, two boards have an embossed *fleur de lis* stamped upon them, the emblem popular in Castine prior to, and after, America's war for independence.

Credit to MLF.

That the house was rebuilt from time to time, always within the same basic frame, is evident by the mix of random and standard size planks in the roof structure and the floors. The hand railing leading upstairs was repositioned in 2018. The newel post at the top of the stairs was prised away from the wall to make room for a steel pole, for stair-climbers to hang onto. The removal of the post revealed an iron nail of a type (rectangular rather than square) forged in the mid-1800s.

Many of the streets within the historic town plat feature at least one heritage Cape Cod on each block. The oldest ones, and likely the first built, stand close to the road. It was town policy in 1785 that houses be "exactly six feet" from the road allowance.

Credit to Emily Somers.

Delivery of drinking water and removal of waste by horse-drawn wagons was easier if houses were two steps away from the curb. The house at #113 stands closer to the road than any of its neighbours in block F. It stands as close to the curb as the Loyalist House one block to the north.

The basement of #113, when first built, would have had a serviceable depth only under the *keeping room* at the back of the house. The half-basement was where vegetables were kept cool in summer and prevented from freezing in winter. The first ice box would not grace the kitchen until the mid-1800s. The keeping room featured a fireplace and kitchen, and would have been the main gathering place.

The interior of the house, and of the oldest neighbouring houses, had the same basic layout: those two generously sized rooms at the front of the house; the keeping room along the back; a small room on one end of the keeping room for storage (that would become an inside bathroom); steep "Captain's Stairs" - favoured by ships' carpenters – from the first to the second floor; and, two rooms upstairs with sloped ceilings. It was *de rigueur* in those days to outfit attic rooms so that sailors from ships anchored in the bay could have places to stay for a night or two. An outhouse was tucked out of sight at the back.

✯✯✯✯✯

When military engineers are involved, house construction is certain to be highly coordinated. Within a year the town counted ninety public buildings, stores, and houses. Four years later, in 1788, the number was six hundred. The construction schedule gave priority in ascending order, from Water Street to Queen, Montague, Parr, Carleton, and up.

John Crafford would have been ready for the arrival of British soldiers at his soon-to-be doorstep. A foundation of layered stones would have been in place. Half hewn posts cut from mature cedar, driven four feet deep into the clay, would have been pre-positioned to receive joists. A five foot deep hole in the ground was dug where the keeping room would be.

While the first houses were being constructed in St. Andrews, in America the Continental Congress almost fell apart (1783 to 1786). The constitution which saved the union of New England colonies was drafted and signed in 1787. In 1789, the man who oversaw its drafting became that country's eighth president – its first president under the new constitution.

The names of the seven men who had served before George Washington have been largely lost to history. Those names, Washington's included, would have been spat out by most UEL between curse words while their fingers froze in winter and while they sweated at their house construction in summer. Not one of them ever expected to homestead a second time in the rugged bush of North America.

PART 3: EARLY TRANSFERS

John Crafford's property was sold during, or shortly after, the War of 1812. The buyer was Edward Parker, a deed merchant and speculator in land. But in a local census for 1816 Timothy Parker and Susannah, Edward's father and mother, are the ones lined up against #113. It suggests Edward bought the house for his parents. Timothy, the father, may have been ill. He died in 1818.

In 1822, after negotiations with the Greenlaw, Cumberland, and Riley families, Edward picked up lot #8 next door as well. Though money was paid to each of the three families in amounts that are on the public record, not all parties were satisfied. This would lead to trouble down the line.

Deals were often done in those days with hand shakes and promises of future exchange. There were myriad disputes. The disputes kept the justices of the peace, the agents of government first appointed by Lieutenant Governor Thomas Carleton, very busy. Appointed JPs, as they were commonly referred to, would rule in St. Andrews until replaced by elected officials in 1877. Distrust of democracy, which underlay the Loyalists' flight from Castine, held sway in New Brunswick for a very long time.

In 1823 Edward sold lots #7 and #8 – "with premises" – to his widowed mother for three-hundred-and-fifty-pounds sterling. He confirmed this in the hand-written transfer document mentioned previously. In that document only John Crafford is noted as a previous owner ("grantee").

✯✯✯✯✯

Edward Parker's family had sailed in 1783 from New York to Saint John.

Timothy Parker, whose dependents at the time were a wife, son Edward, and two other children (six more still to come), had been a soldier. After landing, he signed up with the militia. He was likely called up when a French war ship poked about in the Bay of Fundy in 1795.

There were fifteen other Parkers among the UEL who fled New England, two of whom were members of the Penobscot Association. As was true for generations before and would be true for generations afterward, the success of one family member in a new land persuaded siblings, cousins, nephews, and nieces to follow suit. Over time, by way of descent and immigration, the Parkers became a tribe of their own in New Brunswick. The quirkiest of the lot was *Painless Parker,* a dentist who roamed towns and villages along the Fundy coast in the 1940s and early 1950s. He became a millionaire through the innovative methods – some said quackery – by which he repaired teeth.

Timothy, often partnered with his brother Isaac, transacted for land in Saint John itself (Parr Town) and in the back-lands of at least three counties (Kings, York, and Sunbury). In Saint John, Timothy's full-time profession was listed as *Innkeeper*. As an innkeeper, plugged into food supplies and drink, Timothy doubled as a victualler. He delivered food, wines and water to the ships that sailed between the British and American shores of the Passamaquoddy, the Bay of Fundy, and the Atlantic beyond.

On at least one occasion Timothy needed to go on land in America, requiring him – while the War of 1812 was underway – to take the "Returns of Enemy Aliens" oath. From the beginning of that war political leaders in New Brunswick and in New England had agreed that relations between their respective populations would remain peaceful. The UEL in St. Andrews, and their families in America, had reconciled. Parker promised not take up arms against the new republic.

Credit to Emily Somers.

Timothy was in his sixties when he and Susannah moved from Saint John to St. Andrews. Three of their eight adult children (a ninth child, Thomas, had died at age fifteen) were already residents. Daughter Lydia and son Joseph had married in St. Andrews.

✯✯✯✯✯

In the mid-afternoon of November 7th, 1819, a recently widowed Susannah Parker would have been scared out of her wits on *Dark Sunday*. A meteorological event darkened the sky in southern New Brunswick to a deeper black than the darkest of nights in mid-winter. It happened again two days later, accompanied this time by a sour rain and lightning. There was no eclipse, no volcanic activity, no large fire feeding ash into the air. Many believed the phenomenon signalled the end of the world. Candles were lit in the churches of St. Andrews and Saint John. Farewells were exchanged on the streets among the few who dared step outside.

Credit to Khaled Desouki, Getty Images.

To survive the end of the world Susannah may have leaned upon a neighbour for help. As it happened, lot #6 bordering Edward's property on its immediate left was owned by Archibald McLachlan. Susannah Parker must have known Archibald and his family very well. The unfolding of her story will confirm this.

✭✭✭✭✭

Archibald McLachlan, a stone mason, was born in 1754 in Scotland. He and Rosetta, his wife, sailed from Greenock to North America soon after St. Andrews was incorporated. Their daughter, Julia Ann, was born in St. Andrews in 1787. Sons John and Archibald were born in 1789 and 1793. A third son, George, made the family complete.

Archibald McLachlan, the father, had petitioned for land upon his arrival in 1785. Not being a Loyalist, he was low on the priority list. He did not receive land until 1797. He then used his equity in 180 acres of back-land to buy town lots. In addition to lot #6 in block F, acquired in 1811, he bought a lot in block Q from Elija Greenlaw – a brother of Ebenezer. The deed merchant he relied upon for both transactions was Edward Parker.

Archibald's son John and John's new wife died in 1810. They left a son behind, also named John, who was adopted by Archibald and Rosetta. The boy was baptized in the All Saints Church of St. Andrews in May, 1812. War clouds hovered over the New England states and British colonies in North America at the time. Clouds then gathered over the McLachlans. In 1823, nine years after the *Treaty of Ghent*, Rosetta passed away.

In the year Rosetta died, Susannah accepted a proposal of marriage from Archibald. The two were wed with Susannah's son, Edward, signing their marriage document in the capacity of witness.

Susannah, upon remarriage, became stepmother to her new husband's adult children and to John McLachlan, Archibald's adopted grandson, now a teenager.

Credit to Emily Somers.

As per the laws at the time, Susannah's newly acquired lots #7 and #8 were moved into her second husband's name. Edward may have delayed the sale of properties to his mother with this in mind. Men in those days did not trust the business acumen of women very much. For one thing, few women had access to education beyond the basics of reading and writing.

Young John McLachlan, on the other hand, was likely in his senior year at the Grammar School, at the top of King Street. The school had opened, only for boys, in 1817.

The Grammar School was a two room building with a center hall for combined classes in Latin and Greek. Reverend John Cassilis, a Presbyterian minister who devoted twenty years to his school before returning to the ministry, taught languages (he spoke seven himself) and navigation. Many sailors and sea captains trained in St. Andrews would credit Mr. Cassilis for their ability to read and write, and to know their numbers well enough to plot a course from one seaport to another.

★★★★★

Archibald McLachlan, upon marriage to Susannah, became owner of three contiguous town lots and a house to live in. Archibald also had the back-land granted in 1797, his lot in block Q, twenty acres outside of town purchased from Ebenezer Greenlaw for twenty shillings, and other properties.

However ambitious his plans may have been, in 1824 – a year after marrying Susannah – Archibald McLachlan died. On the same day archival records show that a boy (age six) and a girl (age four), children of George McLachlan, also died. It appears a sickness or accident took away Archibald and two of his grandchildren.

After Archibald's death his acres of back-land were transferred to his daughter Julia Ann, now wife of John McFarlane, a founding member of the Greenock Presbyterian Church on Montague Street. Lots #6, #7, and #8 went to Susannah, once again a widow and once again able to hold property in her own name.

★★★★★

With regard to lot #8 purchased from Ebenezer Greenlaw, remember that Edward Parker had been unable to satisfy all claimants? After Archibald McLachlan's death, William and Sally Greenlaw, son and daughter-in-law of Ebenezer, contested Archibald's estate. A John Cumberland and his wife, Miriam, filed a claim on lot #8 as well.

Ebenezer Greenlaw seems to have been a particularly

querulous sort. He frequently harped upon the burden of his nine dependents and his suffering at the hands of rebels. Though he qualified from the start for a town lot and 100 acres of back-land, for fifty pounds sterling he purchased an additional 100 acres from Moses Sprague. Sprague pursued Greenlaw for non-payment. Greenlaw counter-claimed that Sprague had not cleared the land to the extent promised. It took almost two decades to get the transaction between Sprague and Greenlaw fully implemented. Ebenezer Greenlaw and his family were destined to become major property owners in Charlotte County. Greenlaw Mountain will carry the family name forever.

✮✮✮✮✮

In 1825 Alexander Strachan (merchant/victualler) bought Susannah's lots #6, #7, and the disputed lot #8 for two-hundred-pounds sterling. In the New Brunswick land petitions for 1783 – 1918 a deed is recorded for "land and premise and appurtenances" in his name. The parties who eventually ceded all claims to lot #8 are listed as McLachlan, Greenlaw, Cumberland, and yet another claimant by the name of Collins.

Strachan's eyes turned to lot #5.

In mortgage papers signed by Alexander Strachan in 1829 he wrote that he "now resides" on the four lots – #5, #6, #7, and #8 – along Montague Street. Alexander and his wife Martha (mid-thirties, known to her friends as Patty) lived in the only house that would stand on the north-eastern side of block F in Bulkeley's Division fronting Montague Street until 1865. It appears – because nothing is recorded in this regard – that the Strachans had no children.

One of the children born to St. Andrews while the Strachans lived at #113 was Edwin Bannister, a Black whose father was from Barbados.

At John Cassilis' Grammar School, Edwin stood out for his talent at drawing. When orphaned by the death of his mother (his father died when Edwin was four) he and his brother were given work, plus room and board, on a farm owned by Harris Hatch, one of the wealthiest of the town's citizens. Both boys subsequently went to sea, then took up barbering in the city of Boston. When in Boston, Edwin's drawings attracted the attention that would win him a scholarship to New England art schools. By the late 1800s Bannister paintings had become the rage all along the coast.

When asked late in his life about challenges facing people of colour, Bannister said that British "fair play" had made him feel equal to everyone else when growing up in St. Andrews. He said overt discrimination, which landed him in many a fistfight, became a problem only after he crossed the border into America.

A history of the Greenock Presbyterian Church documents the presence of Alexander Strachan in pew #62 at the first communion held in the Kirk on June 26, 1825. The Kirk was built on the other side of Montague Street, on the corner of Edward Street, visible from the front and side windows of #113.

At their pew, in 1832, the Strachans likely prayed for the salvation of passengers and crew quarantined for fourteen days in the St. Andrews harbour on board *Susan* owing to "cholera morbus". During those two weeks, financed by a two-hundred-pound sterling grant from the province, the town sent staff onto the ship to fumigate and clean. On the streets, face masks were common and social distancing was observed.

Credit to the Provincial Archives of New Brunswick.

Though the epidemic was world-wide and devastating in many places, St. Andrews was largely spared. The good fortune of the town was to be experienced again and again, with every pandemic that followed.

Until his death in 1847, Alexander Strachan must have been a notable presence in St. Andrews. His house stood alone on one of the larger private land holdings – over one full acre – within the town plat. It seems safe to assume that a barn, which shows up in subsequent deed transfers and in early photographs, was built onto the ell at the back of the house during Alexander and Martha Strachan's ownership of all four lots. There was enough land for them to run a small farm in the very centre of town.

In the bell tower above the clock of the Kirk are slatted windows through which, looking west and down, Alexander's house and barn could be seen from a perspective shared only with birds. The Wright brothers would not get the first airplane off the ground for another eighty years.

Credit to St. Andrews Civic Trust.

★★★★★

George McLachlan bought #113 from the widowed Martha Strachan in 1847. George would have known the house from when his father and stepmother lived there. In the deed transfer the property was described as "the north end of lot#7, with buildings". For the purpose of the sale, the bottom half had been severed.

George McLachlan's purchase of the house, barn, and half-lot on which they stood may have been a way for him to help Martha Strachan boost her finances. Martha, with money in her pocket after the sale, stayed put.

★★★★★

Between 1847 and 1850 fifteen thousand people, mostly Protestants from the northern province of Ulster, Ireland, landed at Saint John. The potato famine in that country was just getting started. Many stayed in Saint John for only a week or two, long enough to see that the city was bursting at its seams. Hundreds hurriedly booked passage on ships destined for towns on the coast of the Bay of Fundy and the Atlantic, all the way down to Boston and New York City. Along with the people went their illnesses.

A typhus epidemic was launched that ravaged much of the east coast.

The ship *Star* was the first, in 1850, to show up in the Passamaquoddy Bay waving a yellow flag. It was the signal that typhus was on board. There were three physicians in St. Andrews at the time, nowhere near enough to deal with over sixty victims among 383 passengers.

The captain was ordered to stay at anchor while accommodations were built on a small island in the Bay newly named Hospital Island. Sixty-three people were transferred from the ship to crude huts on the island. The remaining three hundred and twenty were quarantined on board for the duration.

Over the next five years some four hundred Irish immigrants would die of typhus, then smallpox, and then diphtheria on that wretched island. In 1995 a memorial cross overlooking the site was erected by the Irish-Canadian Association of Canada.

Credit to MLF.

The sympathy felt by some on the mainland – Martha Strachan perhaps among them – was trumped many times over by the fear and vigilance of most. The shoreline was patrolled by volunteers to ensure no one boated to the mainland to break quarantine. Homes, commonly referred to as pest houses, were requisitioned along Harriet Street to hold in isolation those who got sick in town.

To locate the pest houses along Harriet Street, of course, was to house the sick just across the road from Slabtown. In census reports of the period Slabtown is described as a mix of shanties (three of these), four "frame shanties", two two-story frames, a log house and a cabin. These modest homes housed fifty-one Black men, women and children.

★★★★★

The year 1865 is notable for Premier Samuel Leonard Tilley's loss in a provincial election to anti-confederation forces. A majority of New Brunswick residents looked south for travel and trade, rather than west – towards the British colonies of Upper and Lower Canada. Eighteen-hundred and sixty-five was also the year when Martha severed lot #8. She then sold the bottom halves of lots #7 and #8. The two half-lots together maintained the municipal standard of 80x160 feet.

The second severance and sale, like the first, may have been done to top up Martha's bank account. There were no pensions for widows in those days.

Richard Waycott, purchaser of the two half-lots, was the son of John and Susan Waycott, Britishers who took their family (eldest son, Henry, was not yet a year old) from England to St. Andrews in 1827. Richard was born in St. Andrews in 1829 and would have four more siblings before his parents were through. He cobbled money together to buy into block F from Patty when he was thirty-five years old.

A town map drawn in 1877 shows a house on the bottom half of lot #8, fronting Edward Street. It is similar in size to other residential homes in the vicinity.

✮✮✮✮✮

While on this tangent, let's peek into the future. Waycott descendants lived in the house Richard built for about sixty years.

✮✮✮✮✮

The Waycott family would run into financial trouble at the front end of the stock market crash that began the Great Depression of the 1930s. Richard's heirs lost the bottom halves of lots #7 and #8 to the Town of St. Andrews.

Twenty-two years later, in 1948, the town sold the former Waycott properties to Russell and Robert Thompson. A two-story building, with residential space on the second floor, replaced Richard Waycott's small Cape Cod. The Thompson brothers ran a taxi and trucking business from their ground-floor garage. A year later the Thompsons exchanged the bottom half of lot #7 for the top half of lot #8 with the then- owners of #113, the Langmaids. Deed #44135, dated 1949, records the transaction that reunited both halves of lot #7. While the lot was made whole again, the severance remained in place.

A family home was built on the top half of lot #8. The house, facing Edward Street, was sold by "old lady Thompson" to Tom and Cathy Partridge at the turn of the twenty-first century. It then sold again, in 2021, to Janice Matthew. Though Janice was from Ontario, she had deep roots in New Brunswick through her father, a McConnell. The McConnells emigrated from Ireland to the Moncton area in 1790.

⭐⭐⭐⭐⭐

Let's now follow the McConnells back into the past.

⭐⭐⭐⭐⭐

It took two years for Britain's Lieutenant Governor, Arthur Gordon, to beat back anti-confederation forces in New Brunswick. He used his position of authority to, in a word, overpower electoral politics. Canada became a country in 1867 and Leonard Tilley – vindicated by the political establishment – was knighted for being a *Father of Confederation*. Two years later, in 1869, Martha Strachan had had enough. She passed away.

George McLachlan's good deed, if that is what it was, had been done. He put this house up for sale.

⭐⭐⭐⭐⭐

In 1870, a self-designated "yeoman" (small land owner, loyal to the Crown) took possession of #113 and the half-portion of lot #7 underneath. He was a Protestant Irishman by the name of Robert Locke. He had likely emigrated from Ireland to New Brunswick between 1845 and 1852, one of many who fled to Canada and America because of the potato famine.

Locke was born in County Down in 1804. In Canada, he lived most of his life (married, five children) on a farm in the parish of St. Patrick just outside of St. Andrews. Robert purchased #113 in his declining years, possibly to be closer to family. He died at sixty-nine, three years after the purchase. He was buried in the St. Stephen Rural Cemetery.

In the sale of "lot #7 (north half)" after Robert's death in 1873, the barn was specifically mentioned for the first time. The barn was mentioned again in a deed transfer in 1884. The barn appears on a rough map of the town plan of St. Andrews dated 1903 and shows up in a 1930s photograph.

⭐⭐⭐⭐⭐

The next owners of #113 were Captain Thomas Adams (master mariner) and his wife Harriet. Though there were many UEL by the name of Adams – Jane Adams is a rare case of a single woman on the Penobscot Association list – the immediate family of Thomas Adams stayed south of the border. When he sold this house, Thomas wrote that his permanent address was Eastport, Maine.

The tenure of Thomas Adams and his wife marked the first return of New Englanders to a property assigned in 1784 to John Crafford, one of their own. Family rifts were, by now, fully healed.

Who knows why the Adams sailed from Eastport to St. Andrews (there were five ferry lines to choose from), or travelled by rail and coach via Calais and St. Stephen, to relocate? Thomas would continue to fish in the same waters as before. Perhaps they were drawn by aggressive advertising all along the coast which described St. Andrews as a place where *miasmas* – stinky air that brought sickness to many towns and cities – were non-existent. In those days Eastport was notorious for the smell of dead fish.

It was an era when "snake oil salesmen" were running rampant all over the United States. It was an era when people knew a lot about sickness but little about prevention or cures. Lung diseases were a particular concern. The reputation of St. Andrews as free of hay fever (and mosquitoes!) would make the place a major draw for decades to come.

⭐⭐⭐⭐⭐

In 1880 the first set of Baileys (the second set arrived a hundred years later) bought #113 from Thomas Adams and his wife. Bailey, like Adams, is a name common on both sides of the

Maine/New Brunswick border. Baileyville lies across the river from St. Stephen, at the place where two Bailey brothers founded a textile mill in the early 1700s. The first Baileys manufactured cloth and sold clothing. A Joseph Bailey went north with the British in 1783. He was on the list of justices of the peace appointed by Sir Guy Carleton in 1783 to help run St. Andrews.

A John Bailey opened a clothing store on Water Street in the early-1800s. John, a Methodist, must have had Presbyterian leanings because two of his children are buried in the graveyard beside the Kirk. His business, John Bailey and Sons Ltd, was taken over by a surviving son.

Ephraim was not one of *those* Baileys, the ones whose presence in North America had begun in the 1700s. Ephraim emigrated from Tottenham, England, in 1848. For the next thirty-two years he made his home in Saint John. Along the way, in 1863, he married Mary Anne, a young woman from New England. They had a son a year later who they named Wendell.

In 1877 a disastrous fire destroyed a great many public and commercial buildings in Saint John, and many private homes. Ephraim's place of work and house may have been among them.

Three years after the fire, Ephraim took his family to St. Andrews. There he found a job at John Bailey and Sons Ltd. The textile trade seems to have run in the blood of this family.

Four years later #113 Montague Street was sold by Mary Anne Bailey, the third New Englander after John Crafford and Thomas Adams to own the property. When selling her house, the law required Mary Anne to have the transfer documents co-signed by her son, now twenty-one years old. Her husband, Wendell's father, was either dead and gone, or just gone.

Credit to Toronto Public Library.

On the one hand, the deed transfer shows #113 awarded to Mary Anne in Ephraim's will. On the other hand, Loyalist records show that an Ephraim Bailey arrived in Renfrew, Ontario, from New Brunswick in 1883. If it is the same Ephraim, the scoundrel abandoned his wife and son to live out his life on the Ottawa River. His will may have been the only document available to lawyers to dispose of his assets.

The house sold for four-hundred-and-eighty-pounds sterling. The price was paid with a down payment of three-hundred-pounds plus twenty-pounds annually for six years. This was a way in pre-mortgage days to make real estate affordable. Mary Anne moved back to America, to Anoka in Minnesota, with a small nest egg and six years of steady income.

PART 4:
PERSEVERANCE THROUGH CHANGE

The 1884 buyers of #113 were James Randolph (Randolph) Langmaid and Sarah Ellen McCoubrey. Sarah Ellen had family close by, in the graveyard of the Kirk. The McCoubrey plot was at one end of a row marked on the other end by the grave of John Cassilis.

Credit to MLF.

The eight and a half decades of Langmaid ownership were a period of global unrest. The assassination of Czar Alexander III by the brother of Vladimir Lenin, the sinking of the Titanic, the Russian Revolution, two World Wars, the Great Depression, the Korean War, most of the "Cold War", the assassination of President John F. Kennedy, the civil rights movement in America, and domestic strife in Canada that included passage of a War Measures Act.

★★★★★

Randolph was born in St. Andrews in 1854. Langmaid, derived from lang-mead (meaning long meadow) in the area of Devon in southern England, is one of the most ancient Anglo-Saxon names. By descendancy in New Brunswick and by additional immigration the Langmaids, like the Parkers and others, were to become a large family cohort.

Randolph, like his father (also born in St. Andrews, in 1826), probably learned reading and writing, and basic navigation, at Cassilis' Grammar School. The elder Langmaid would have been a student while Cassilis still taught. Both father and son were subsequently trained to be carpenters on board ships.

When sailing as third mate on a ship that rounded the Cape of Good Hope, Randolph and another brave soul allowed themselves to be dangled over the ship's sides during a violent storm in order to lash the breaking tiller in place. The captain of the ship reported that all on board were otherwise doomed.

Randolph left the sea at thirty years of age. He likely had no choice. By the 1880s opportunities for sailors had become few and far between. A major pivot in transportation technologies – from wood and sail, to iron and steam – had arrived. In Great Britain, the industrial revolution had been running roughshod over gentler technologies for fifty years.

The pivot from wind to coal-fired engines had a profound impact on St. Andrews and all of its residents. Perhaps ship builders and traders in St. Andrews could have adapted? The imperative to do so, however, did not arise. Railways were already carrying more wealth into town than shipbuilding and trade ever did.

Credit to Emily Somers/Charlotte County Archives.

The railway carried a cohort of visitors for whom money was no object. They were people who could easily afford the luxury of a sleeping car from as far away as New York City, Chicago, or Toronto. They could buy and sell the locals many times over. They could take entire summers off. They built resplendent summer "cottages" for their families. They shifted the employment base of St. Andrews from ship building to house construction, to gardening, to plumbing, electrical wiring, and to other services.

*Credit to Emily Somers,
with permission of Dominion Hill Country Inn.*

The newcomers were American and Canadian investors in the St. Andrews Land Company, a company created by Frank Cram and Robert Gardiner. Though Sir Leonard Tilley – retired from politics, and a summer resident of St. Andrews – was its titular head, the Land Company was headquartered on Federal Street in Boston.

Cram was an American from Bangor, Maine, who had come to St. Andrews for the first time in 1885. Already a general manager of the European and North American Railroad headquartered in New England, he was hired to run the fledgling New Brunswick-Quebec line as well.

Gardiner, vice-president of the Rand Avery Supply Company and president of the New England Railway Publishing Company, knew St. Andrews from his frequent visits by yacht beginning in the 1870s. Early meetings of the Land Company were held over dinners at Gardiner's private club.

For St. Andrews, the Land Company had in mind a recreational spot to rival Bar Harbour in Maine. High on their list of projects was the construction of a world-class hotel. The Algonquin, at the top of Prince of Wales Street, opened in 1889. It was a timber-framed structure with two hundred sumptuous suites, clean water that flowed hot and cold, up-to-date plumbing for a tub and toilet in the bathroom of each room, and three generators to provide electric power. The generators powered arc lighting along streets leading up to the hotel, and soon would power the entire town.

★★★★★

Randolph Langmaid exchanged carpentry on board ships for construction jobs on land, likely including work on the Algonquin Hotel. From there, as a self-designated "gardener", he branched into work in the elaborate gardens of the mansions he may have helped to build. In later census reports, he described himself as a general labourer. On occasion he acknowledged himself to be unemployed.

Randolph retired in 1920, at the age of sixty-six. In retirement he declared his income to be fifteen-hundred-pounds a year. A portion of that income was likely earned by his wife, a weaver. Sarah Ellen was known around town for her skill as a seamstress.

She may have been one of the seventy workers who supplied knitted products to the *Cottage Craft* enterprise launched by Helen Mowat in 1914.

Mowat's enterprise reached its peak during the First World War, when *Cottage Craft* responded to the demand for warm clothing from troops in Europe. The business stayed viable under her management until the mid-1940s. The business was sold and carried on for another half-century, in a heritage building at the town wharf.

★★★★★

Randolf and Sarah Ellen had two children. William Norman, who would grow up to work for the same people as his father, was born in 1883. Daughter Sarah Josephine was born in 1886. The iron spike pulled out of a newel post in 2018 may have been driven in by Randolph. If the kids were consigned to the upstairs bedrooms, Father would have wanted a proper banister to keep his children safe.

For the first and only time, tiny voices echoed within the walls of #113. No owners of the house other than the Langmaids had small children while living there. The Cape exchanged hands between seniors, or was purchased by couples as a second home, or was bought by professionals who were just passing through. John McLachlan was already a teenager when his grandfather (and adoptive father) married Susannah Parker. The Strachans, an exception on all three counts (neither seniors, nor part-time residents, nor short-term), were childless.

★★★★★

William Norman was thirteen and his sister only ten when they fretted along with everyone else about the alleged murder of Mr. Michael McMonagle. The daring young man was swamped as he paddled from St. Andrews, where he worked in a foundry, to Eastport. His death was deemed suspicious when the two men who tried to save him were suspected instead of taking his canoe and leaving him to drown. They were tried in Maine. The case was eventually thrown out of court, but it was a *cause celebre* for many months among gossipers. The two accused were of Indigenous ancestry, likely targeted for their race.

Credit to the Charlotte County Archives.

One thing for sure, because McMonagle's body eventually washed up on shore, he had not been eaten by a snake. The summer of the drowning was the same summer a monster snake was seen knifing through the waters of the St. Andrews harbour. Like the Loch Ness monster, resident in a lake in the highlands of Scotland close to where John Crafford was born, the snake reappeared from time to time, haunting the thoughts of children and recreational boaters. Its last appearance happened to be in the only year that wolves were spotted at the edge of a somewhat jittery town.

★★★★★

By the time of Randolph's death, most men and women of working age had become, directly or indirectly, servants of the rich. Son William Norman may even have followed his employers in the off-season (late fall, winter, and spring) to their residence in Montreal. Or did he follow his girlfriend? It was in that city that William Norman married Clara Amelia Innes, born in St. Andrews. Their son, Kenneth, was born in Montreal in 1915. On the birth certificate William states his occupation to be truck driver.

As a toddler Kenneth spent summers in St. Andrews with his paternal grandparents. The lore around grandfather's escapades at sea must have made the old man quite a hero in his grandson's eye.

In 1918 and 1919 St. Andrews provided the little boy and his parents safe haven from the Spanish Flu that was having a devastating impact globally. New Brunswick had acted early, imposing mask-wearing imperatives, social distancing, and the closure of most public and commercial buildings. Though the autocratic JPs were long gone, most New Brunswickers were still quick to do what their political leaders told them to do. St. Andrews was able to maintain its reputation as a healthy place to be.

The family of three – William, Clara, and Kenneth – moved permanently from Montreal back to St. Andrews in 1926 when Kenneth was in grade school. The house at #113, with both grandparents still living, must have been a little crowded! Perhaps this was when the back wall on the second floor was punched out. One of the two bedrooms was enlarged. This may have been when the upstairs toilet and sink were added. Teased by the splendour of the Algonquin, indoor plumbing had become every homeowner's dream. Both Randolph and William Norman had learned how to make it happen.

★★★★★

Randolph left #113 to his widow, son, and daughter in his will. Randolph's death certificate listed the causes of his death to be chronic endocarditis – an infection in the heart cavity – and senility. The year was 1931.

By then daughter Sarah Josephine had married a man by the name of Turner and lived in East Lynn, Massachusetts. There were a dozen Turners listed as members of the Penobscot Association. This suggests daughter Sarah Josephine married into a family that, like most Loyalist families, had maintained deep roots along the east coast of the United States. Relatives were travelling south and north across the border with ease.

Sarah Ellen and Sarah Josephine conferred sole ownership of #113 upon William Norman in 1940. A second world war, which began only months after King George VI and his Queen were waved away from the Saint John harbour by a truck load of St. Andrews admirers, was underway. William Norman – too old at fifty-six – and Kenneth – an only son – were spared service on the front lines.

World War Two was as much a boon for industry in Charlotte County as the previous Great War had been. Britain, still the "mother country" in the minds of many, chose St. Andrews to build one of four *Fundy Class* minesweepers. Dilapidated facilities at Indian Point were hastily refurbished. Immediately after the war the ships would be sold to China and used as tug boats.

The Langmaids must have been as relieved as everyone else when the war finally ended. All employers in the town, and the town itself, gave their staffs two days off to celebrate. Hundreds gathered on the town square in front of the Kennedy Inn. The crowd was entertained by martial music. The people cheered themselves hoarse when Adolph Hitler was hung in effigy.

Those times still had their barbaric moments. When, shortly after the war, two brothers were hung in Fredericton for the murder of a taxi driver, dozens of St. Andrews residents – men and women – joined the throng of thousands who travelled to the capital city to watch.

Sarah Ellen would not have been among them.

Mother Sarah Ellen died at home in 1947, at the age of ninety-two. She likely rests near her parents in the cemetery alongside the Kirk, kitty-corner to the house where she had lived most of her life. Only the headstones of her father, and two siblings who died young, were still legible in 2021.

In 1951, William Norman reassigned #113 Montague and both halves of lot #7 to himself and his wife. Sparked by the 1929 Privy Council decision in the Persons Case, women's rights in Canada were on a roll. The first woman senator – Cairine Wilson, who had a vacation home just outside of St. Andrews – was appointed in 1930. The presumption of joint ownership, however, would not be entrenched in Canadian law until Murdoch vs. Murdoch in 1975. William Norman was a man ahead of his times.

✶✶✶✶✶

Ten years later, in 1961, the top half of lot #7 and the house upon it were transferred to Kenneth Langmaid for one dollar by his father and mother. In the deed the bottom half of the lot is scratched out. If the parents Langmaid wanted to be generous to their son with the top half of the property, with the bottom half they did what they could to supplement their retirement income. They sold the bottom half back to the Thompsons.

After his primary and secondary schooling in St. Andrews, Kenneth had obtained a BSc and MSc at the University of New Brunswick. Along the way he married Dorothy McCurdy, a local girl who followed him by two years in age and grade.

Dorothy McCurdy descended from men and women who had been passengers in the fleet that transported UEL from Castine. Her health, unfortunately, was a constant concern. Early in their marriage she contracted tuberculosis, a disease that was a leading cause of death of young people in Canada at the time. For as long as her health held, Dorothy lived with her husband in the cities where he worked. Business trips that took Kenneth into the field would be occasions for Dorothy to move in with her parents, in St. Andrews.

Kenneth was a pedologist by profession – a scientist who studies soil as a component of natural systems. He was therefore the third generation in a family whose work had ties to the cultivation of plants. Kenneth spent most of his professional life in Ottawa and Fredericton. He taught at schools, sat on boards and commissions, and did his own research. He founded New Brunswick's Conservation Coalition. He was the first owner of #113 whose income was not dependent upon the local economy. For him and Dorothy, this house was a part-time residence.

Kenneth Langmaid was consulted until well into his eighties by governments and big business – the Irving family of Saint John (one of the "summer people") among them. Kenneth Langmaid was at the front-end of what would become the "green" revolution.

✶✶✶✶✶

In 1969, Kenneth followed the example of his father and moved title of #113 into the names of both himself and his wife. They sold this place, which had stayed their second home, in 1970. When Kenneth retired in 1975 he and Dorothy moved from Fredericton into a house on the corner of Montague and William Streets.

Both Langmaids were active in the community. Kenneth sat on numerous boards and committees advising the town on planning and recreational policy. They were also known for the care of rescued animals. Dorothy had joined the Society for the Prevention of Cruelty to Animals when she was in grade two.

Dorothy passed away in 2003, having spent the last decade of her life at the Passamaquoddy Lodge, a home for seniors. Kenneth sat on the board of the Lodge while he continued living at their home in town. After Dorothy's death Kenneth moved to the Lodge and lived three more years.

Credit to MLF.

The impact of Kenneth and Dorothy Langmaid upon St. Andrews was of such significance that a park is named in his honour. The park is close to Indian Point at the end of Water Street.

The St. Andrews Community Foundation still manages the *Dorothy and Kenneth Langmaid Scholarship Fund*, awarded annually to a UNB student who has graduated from a Charlotte County school and has completed the first year in a Bachelor of Science program. There is also a scholarship worth ten to twelve thousand dollars a year for the study of forest soils and tree growth at the post-graduate level. An animal welfare fund supports the work of the SPCA in southwest New Brunswick and in Saint John.

★★★★★

The significance of the Langmaid round of ownership of #113 Montague Street is worth highlighting.

First: it was – and would remain – the only round from the year of its construction that the house hosted little children. A large family might have wanted to tear the place down and build bigger.

Second: with the advent of the Land Company, St. Andrews had become a feudal town. The Algonquin Hotel was its castle on a hill. The "summer residents" were its lords and ladies.

Third: the shift in profession of the Langmaids – from sea, to land – mirrored the shift in St. Andrews' economic base.

Fourth: though the family lived below an invisible line separating wealthy and upper-income families from everyone else, Kenneth achieved special recognition. In return, he and Dorothy left bequests that will benefit St. Andrews and its residents for a very long time.

PART 5: HOP SCOTCH

To play hop scotch is to skip from place to place. After being a refuge for permanent residents for two-hundred-and-twenty years, this house became a home for out-of-town owners and renters. No resident after William Norman depended upon the local economy for income.

The hop scotch players were a different breed from the "summer people" who had come as a group. A long-term resident who was a young woman in the 1950s observed: "We learned so much from the summer people, especially about fashion. We had little to do with them, of course, but they were nice. They had the money to go anywhere in the world. They chose St. Andrews. It made us feel that our town was special."

The newcomers after 1970 chose St. Andrews for reasons that varied from one to the other. They did not bring surplus wealth. After the Langmaids, there would be no bequests, no scholarships, no public parks left behind in their names.

✦✦✦✦✦

In 1970 the house at #113 Montague Street was sold to Gorman Fountain, the fourth New Englander (after Crafford, Adams, and Mary Anne Bailey) to own the property. The primary place of residence of the Fountains remained Worcester, Massachusetts.

While the sale broke a chain of ownership within the Langmaid family that had lasted 86 years, an even older link to St. Andrews may have been re-established. Fountain is a Loyalist name. A Stephen and a Thomas Fountain, both blacksmiths, were two of the first Loyalists to arrive on the shores of the River St. John back in 1783.

Credit to Saint John Real Estate Board

★★★★★

For what reason would a Boston-area resident choose St. Andrews over options all along the coast of Cape Cod?

The sea in the Bay of Fundy is frigid to the point of being un-swimmable – except for crazy kids and a few older stalwarts. The water in Katy's Cove, below the Algonquin Hotel, is different. There, a dyke traps incoming tides long enough for the sun to make a difference. In a tourism brochure of the mid-1900s, sea water along the coasts of New Brunswick – St. Andrews and Katy's Cove are specifically named – was described as the warmest in all of Canada.

New River Beach is a forty-five-minute drive by car from St. Andrews. Sandy? Check. Expansive? Check. Great vistas? Check. Nice place for a picnic? Check. But New River Beach is no match to the sand, sun and surf accessible to families in New England. The whales seen from tour boats based in St. Andrews are the same whales that swim close to the shores of Eastport and Portland in Maine. An hour-long shopping experience along Water Street pales when compared to five minutes in the town of Freeport.

Family history? Family lore? Yes, indeed. That is where St. Andrews has few peers.

For an American to be in St. Andrews, whether for a two-week summer holiday or for months at a time, is to live in the skin of a relative. A great many houses are exactly those first built by refugees who left families behind in Massachusetts and Maine. The streets run exactly the same way as they did when first laid out in 1784, though now paved and slightly wider. The ditches on either side of the roads are those that drained horse manure way back when #113 was built. Every street in town is still named what it was named in 1784, covers the land area it did back then, carries home owners and visitors to the same places and past the same landmarks as ever before.

There have been changes here and there. The original Catholic church burned down, the odd house has been rolled from one location to another, graveyards long ago closed their gates to newly deceased, businesses on Water Street have changed owners, the Algonquin Hotel has been renovated a few times. But not a single Loyalist refugee ghost, if returned to St. Andrews for a visit, would lose its way.

No horse? No problem. No carriage? No problem. John Crafford didn't need either one. No car? No problem. The Langmaids went everywhere on foot. To every house on the peninsula, the downtown of St. Andrews has always been accessible within a fifteen-minute walk. To residents of #113, the trajectory takes only five minutes.

Credit to MLF.

Alexander Strachan, if reborn, might feel claustrophobic because his widow sold parts of his hard-earned property to others. His adjustment inside the closed door of #113 Montague Street, however, would be swift. He would just love the larger windows, the two fancy toilets, the comfortable central heating, the backyard patio. He would surely forgive Patty for the encumbrances she allowed. She needed the money to live out her years.

On a Sunday morning, Alexander Strachan could again take his seat in pew #62. Everything about that church, outside and in, is still today what it was in 1825. The cross-streets, Edward and Montague, were paved in 1937 but that's about it.

✭✭✭✭✭

In 1977, after a one-hundred year absence, the Baileys returned. Richard and Lucie Bailey bought #113 Montague Street for $25,000 and stayed for two years. They likely had no idea why they felt so much at home.

Richard, a researcher posted by Canada's Department of Fisheries and Oceans to the Biological Research Centre at the edge of town, was on a short-term assignment. In 1978, Richard Bailey published a study on the status of snow crabs in the Gulf of St. Lawrence.

Credit to Emily Somers.

Snow crabs, which get their name from the colour of the meat, live in the North Atlantic and North Pacific waters. Their spawn fill water columns after spilled from female crabs, sink to the bottom of the cold oceans, and live for some twenty years. In the course of those years they grow by shedding one shell and building another until the point of full maturity is reached. Snow crabs have homes too!

✯✯✯✯✯

Richard Bailey's arrival in St. Andrews followed on the heels of Donald Small, also a scientist, who had come from Castine on a short-term teaching contract. The Huntsman Marine Science Centre, having launched an aquaculture training program in 1974, needed help. Small rented an apartment above The Leather Store on Water Street for his family of four. At the end of his contract, Small returned to his teaching position at the Maine Maritime Academy. He left behind a town in which the number of residents with a Doctoral degree was said to be higher per capita than anywhere else in Canada.

Small's daughter, a child at the time, remembered St. Andrews with great affection. Karen, holding a position with the Castine town council in 2021, observed how Castine and St. Andrews were so much alike. Over two hundred years after the former birthed the latter with a transfer of people and houses, the comparison between the two coastal towns remained strong.

✯✯✯✯✯

Richard and Lucie Bailey were able to discharge their mortgage because James and Hilda Little bought #113 in 1979. Little is a Loyalist name.

Along the road from St. Andrews to Fredericton, which was deemed a highway when broadened for two stagecoaches to pass abreast in the mid-1800s, the name "Little" appears on signs everywhere. Briggs and Little is a major wool producer in New Brunswick, with an international reputation.

A nephew of Richard and Lucie said that his uncle and aunt came to St. Andrews to enjoy an affordable retirement. They were both enthusiastic gardeners. The nephew, only a baby in 1979, went into gardening as a business when he grew up. He would be hired forty years later to help the owners of the day keep the gardens around #113 in good order.

Hilda was widowed in 1984. She would live on her own for twenty more years.

For the Town of St. Andrews, 1984 was a year of poignancy and celebration. A poignant moment came when citizens gathered to wave good-bye to Engine #8027. The rail link between the town and the rest of New Brunswick was shut down. In October, most eyes were glued to television to see Canada's first astronaut – Marc Garneau – take off into space. His mother was one of five Richardson sisters who went to the same high school as Kenneth Langmaid and Dorothy McCurdy. Marc's grandmother, still residing in St. Andrews, was among those invited to Cape Canaveral to witness the lift-off.

Also in 1984, by yacht, Great Britain's Prince Charles and his Princess came to see the town where his grandmother had opened St. Andrews' Centennial Gardens. Black bunting, to mourn the tragic death of Lady Diana, hung on the front of many houses and businesses thirteen years later.

When the "War on Terror" followed destruction of the Twin Towers in New York City, Hilda Little must have been comforted by the isolation of this town from the world outside. St. Andrews is a bit of a Brigadoon. Everyone who visits is charmed. Smiles on peoples' faces – when not hidden by face masks! – are a characteristic of this place. The cares of the world can be left behind.

✮✮✮✮✮

The Pillons – Kenneth and Christine – bought from Hilda Little in 2004 and retained ownership for four years. They knew the town from visits to the summer "cottage" of a friend.

An unhappy event during the Pillon years was the closing of the St. Andrews Hockey Academy, a school that had attracted international attention over its forty-two years of existence. To see National Hockey League players and coaches saunter down from the Algonquin Hotel had been common. In one summer, twenty-five hundred kids participated in that season's many hockey camps.

The house at #113 was once again a part-time residence. The Pillons lived at 75 Orange Street in Saint John, in a heritage three-story townhouse of Queen Anne Revival and Italianate design. The townhouse was built by Edward Mooney in 1880, the same year Ephraim Bailey moved with Mary Anne and Wendell to St. Andrews, which was three years after the devastating fire of 1877.

It may have been during the tenure of the Pillons that the interior of #113 was significantly upgraded. The guts of the building were torn out. Rooms were opened up. A high-quality fireplace and chimney were built into the wall of the living room. The kitchen acquired a modern look and feel appropriate for the early 2000s. It is the kind of work that one with an eye for style does in a hobby house. The Pillons could stay home in Saint John while the insides of #113 were ripped apart.

At the side of the house, further back from the street, a garage was built. Between the house and the garage an enclosed courtyard was fancied up by the laying down of a large flag-stone patio. On a sunny day in February one could sit close to the house in that courtyard and enjoy a tanning experience.

Credit to MLF.

★★★★★

Patrick and Marcia McManaman bought from the Pillons in 2008, at the tail end of the biggest stock market collapse since the Great Depression. The price of houses in all of New Brunswick was rock bottom.

The "War on Terror" somewhat abated, the McManamans spent winter months in the Middle East, where Patrick worked on contract. In the summers Marcia was committed to gardening. She is the one who gave to #113 its name, *Once Upon a Time*. It was a name that neighbours found endearing. Perhaps Marcia sensed that the house was poised to tell its stories?

Though neither Patrick nor Marcia were sailors, the St. Andrews Yacht Club was a favoured place. Marcia took a position on the board of the club as secretary. The veranda at the back of the club, overlooking the Passamaquoddy Bay, would have been a great spot to toast the sighting of a Great White shark in 2014. It was also a great place for club members to savour the different varieties of wine the McManamans brewed as a hobby. Rows of empty wine bottles were left stacked in the unfinished basement of #113 when title next changed hands.

At #113, new windows were installed all around. An insert went into the recently-built fireplace in the living room. The garage was upgraded into a work shop. The concrete floor of the garage received an insulated press-board surface, the roof was re-shingled and a chimney was built into it. A pot-bellied stove was intended. Marcia planned to use the garage in all four seasons as a painter's studio when Patrick fully retired.

In 2015, however, Patrick was injured in a car accident. For two years Marcia devoted her time in St. Andrews to his care. The garden was left unattended. The pot-bellied stove was not procured.

★★★★★

In 2017 Rem Westland, a Dutchman born in Indonesia, and Marie La Forest, daughter of two New Brunswickers, took over.

Rem, a classmate of Marc Garneau at the Royal Military College of Canada, came to find his feet as a writer. Marie came to be closer to her father, who lived in Fredericton. Both had earned a pension after thirty years with the federal government's military and public service, and from work as consultants.

Through her mother, Marie's roots went back three generations in Saint John. A heritage sign featuring the name of a great-great uncle, a butcher, still hangs large on the wall of the Saint John Market. Marie's father was a *Brayon* from Grand Falls. His ancestors may date as far back as the French expedition in 1604 to Isle St. Croix. The family name appears in accounts regarding the Sieur de la Salle, who awarded Belle Island in Lake Ontario to his lawyer, M. La Forest, in the late 1600s. Marie was a lawyer, as had been her father. Two sisters, a step-daughter, and a son were lawyers as well.

Two years of inattention had left the garden at the side and back of the house in total disarray. Making things worse, an extension of the highway between Saint John and St. Stephen had cut off habitat for deer in the area. Deer on the St. Andrews side were stuck.

All plants edible by deer, most noticeably all cedar bushes, had been eaten to the height that a deer could reach in winter. Each year, the ravenous deer adjusted their diets. Rhododendrons were ignored for a while. After the lower four feet of mature cedars were gone, however, the Rhododendrons were next up. Even tiny leaves surrounded by the lethal thorns of bramble bushes became the target of winter-time feeding.

A dominant issue for the town was the management of its housing stock. Many houses – #113 among them – were owned by out-of-towners while locals were desperate for an affordable place to live. A second issue was the burgeoning deer population – a tremendous draw for tourists but a scourge for gardeners. How to prepare for the impact of climate change was a third.

Credit to MLF.

Though hedging their bets by retaining property in Ontario, Rem and Marie intended their move to be permanent. They attended town council meetings when publicly held, signed up for boards and committees, and were regulars at local events. Through Marie's membership on the board of the Archives they researched and wrote content for banners that were installed in the Charlotte County Court House to say what happened in that place. In early summer and late fall, if not at their cottage on Sharbot Lake, they biked the Van Horne Trail to Katy's Cove for a swim.

Then came the 2020 pandemic. A novel coronavirus, Covid-19, unleashed action by governments marked by restrictions to the freedoms of association and movement. To combat the scepticism of some, *follow the science* became the battle cry of most.

As did the fear of other diseases since the arrival of *Susan* in the early 1800s, fear of infection limited physical contact among humans outside private homes. Pedestrians crossed the road rather than pass someone else on the sidewalk, especially if that other person was not wearing a face mask. In a country that had never had its internal borders policed, travel between provinces became difficult. Cross-border travel by car between Canada and the United States was stopped altogether.

Credit to CBC News.

Once again, there was little sickness in Charlotte County. The reputation of St. Andrews as a healthy place was maintained. This had a significant impact upon real estate: houses were moved off the bed-and-breakfast market to be sold like hot cakes to buyers from out-of-province, from America as far away as San

Francisco, and from overseas. Prices rose dramatically. Permanent residents were squeezed even more.

Though the grip of Canada's federal and provincial governments would loosen when vaccines hit the market, the message to Canadians had been clear: pick a spot, and stay there! An infringement of individual rights by governments, done once, gets easier to do again. Experts sternly advised that future pandemics were certain.

For Rem and Marie, as between New Brunswick and Ontario, freedom on the six acres of their property in Ontario – closer to their adult children – was the more compelling alternative. The banners in the courthouse, the text of by-laws written for the Charlotte County Archives, Rem's novel, and the stories of this house would be the legacy of their time in St. Andrews.

AFTERWORD

In the years to come, how many more stories will this house be around to tell?

Houses are vulnerable. However loyally a house may serve, for however long, its residents come and go. Tastes change. Old houses collapse upon themselves. Sometimes they are burned to the ground by accident. Sometimes they are sacrificed, on purpose, to progress. For consultants who advise governments, the staying-power of a house depends upon relevance.

From the day of its construction to the years of the Langmaids, #113 was, above all, an affordable refuge for permanent residents. This little Cape looked on, with awe, when the mansions of the "summer people" arrived.

John Crafford was not a rich man. After Crafford, Edward Parker was a deed merchant who needed a safe place for his father, who was ill. Susannah, Edward's mother, briefly owned the home when widowed. Her re-marriage, to Archibald McLachlan, must have been a tremendous relief in an era when few women had the means to live alone.

Alexander Strachan appears to have had the money to purchase a more imposing house than #113, but his eye was also on land. After pulling all four lots between Edward and Elizabeth Streets together, Alexander splurged to build a barn rather than a larger home. After his death, his widow, Martha, severed and sold half of lots #7 and #8. She must have needed the money. Martha Strachan was lucky to have the friendship and the advice of George McLachlan, son of Archibald and Rosetta.

Robert Locke, an Irishman who fled the potato famine, was elderly (for those days) when he sold his farm in nearby St.

Patrick parish to buy this place. He died at the age of sixty-nine, only three years after moving in.

Captain Thomas Adams, from Maine, could continue to fish in the waters of the Passamaquoddy and the Bay of Fundy after he and his wife took over. He would have spent surplus cash on his boat. He and Harriet returned seven years later to a house in Eastport they perhaps had never sold.

Ephraim Bailey fled with his wife and son from a burnt-out Saint John. Ephraim found work with extended family in the clothing business, suggesting he may have lost everything he owned in the *great fire*. Randolph Langmaid, who moved into #113 with his wife after Ephraim died or ran away, was – as had been his father – a carpenter on wooden sailing ships. Theirs was a trade without a future.

In the last decade of the Langmaid's eighty-six years of ownership, #113 evolved from being an affordable home for permanent residents into a house – often a second home – for people whose lives were also lived elsewhere. Periods of tenure got shorter. The skipping from owner to owner, the hop scotch, began when Kenneth Langmaid and his wife Dorothy stayed in Fredericton.

The Fountains, Baileys, Pillons, McManamans, and Westland/La Forest held the place as a part-time residence or were often out of town. James and Hilda Little were an exception, coming here to retire.

After twenty-five years in the hands of the Littles, twenty of these with Hilda widowed, this house – inside and out – must have been worn out. Humans and houses, if they age together, often deteriorate apace.

The Pillons and McManamans appear to have had the money

to tear down #113 and start over. Yet both sets of owners, and then the Westland/La Forest duo, elected to rebuild within the same frame. Why? Did the Pillons value the history of #113? Did Patrick and Marcia feel a connection to previous owners? Perhaps the house whispered to them, as it did to Rem and Marie: *I deserve to be saved.*

But by what right can #113 ask to be saved? What makes this little place special? The Dunns, Maxwells, Hosmers, and their wealthy cohort would not have looked twice.

St. Andrews has witnessed parts of itself be dismantled many times since 1783. In the mid-twentieth century an entire block of buildings, the O'Neill corner on Water Street, was taken away. An old Cape on Queen Street was taken down, the lot landscaped, and all trace removed within a week. As the world steps hesitantly into a "green" future, what will happen to loyal structures like #113?

This house cannot measure up to contemporary boxes of steel and plastic, with their triple-pane thermal windows, powered by the sun, insulated to remain cool in summer and warm in winter. With its small footprint on the north-eastern half of lot #7, this house hogs a property that could hold a home large enough for two families or more. Available housing for permanent residents on the peninsula has been at a premium since St. Andrews was founded.

In 2017 the St. Andrews Civic Trust led an initiative to have the town council adopt a heritage by-law. The Charlotte County Archives were in full support. Though all of St. Andrews had been declared a national historic site twenty years earlier, the initiative failed.

A heritage by-law would be a collective response to the

whispered plea of places like #113. It is a plea that must have come from the O'Neill corner of buildings on Water Street. It must have come from that tiny Cape on Queen Street.

Old buildings, after all, are more than their component parts. They incorporate the lives of the people who lived in them. Old houses are monuments to families past, going back centuries. To walk by newly vacant land in the town core of St. Andrews is to feel an inexplicable sadness.

The stories of this house have been told in the hope that its plea for protection will always be heard. Coffee table books about the history of St. Andrews never depict #113 Montague Street or mention any of its residents. The house is not celebrated for architectural style. It is a courageous little place that has nonetheless held its own from the very beginning.

Credit to MLF.

INVENTORY OF SOURCES

1. St. Andrews: An Historical Scrapbook (edited by David Sullivan, 2008)
2. Charlotte County Archives: various files and films
3. A Brief Early History of Castine (David M. Van Horn, 1993)
4. Salt Water Town: Stories of Castine, Maine (Donald Small, 2016)
5. The Loyalists of New Brunswick (Esther Clark Wright, 2003)
6. The Diverting History of a Loyalist Town (Grace Helen Mowat, 1953)
7. Land of the Loyalists (Ronald Rees, 2000)
8. New Brunswick: An Illustrated History (Ronald Rees, 2014)
9. Historic St. Andrews: Images of our Past (Ronald Rees, 2001, 2007)
10. Peoples of the Maritimes: Blacks (Bridglal Pachai, 1993)
11. Know New Brunswick: The Essential History (Dan Soucoup, 2009)
12. Source Materials Relating to the New Brunswick Indian (edited by W. D. Hamilton and W. A. Spray, 1977)
13. A Neighbourly War: New Brunswick and the War of 1812 (Robert L. Dallison, 2012)
14. The Aroostook War of 1839 (W. E. Campbell, 2013)
15. Summers in St. Andrews (Willa Walker, 1982, 2006)
16. Imaginary Line (Jacques Poitras, 2011)
17. The Evolution of the Cape Cod House (Arthur P. Richmond, 2011)

About the Author

Rem Westland turned to writing after a career in the Canadian Forces, academia, public service, consulting, and politics. He has self-published two books. *Running for the People* is about his run for Canada's parliament in the 2011 federal election. *Badly Hidden* is a novel about a soldier who causes the death of his wife during a PTSD event. *Nobody Cares* (TotalRecall Publications, 2021), on the subject of power abuse, is set in St. Andrews. A number of short stories on the theme of entitlement have been published by Ottawa Independent Writers.

ONCE UPON A TIME

At the close of the 1700s, a refugee who fled with his family from Castine, Maine, to St. Andrews in New Brunswick was granted the property that these stories are about. John Crafford was one of 643 members of the Penobscot Association, evacuated by sea in 1783. There were tens of thousands of other men, women, and children desperate to escape the American Revolution. They had good reason to be afraid. In France, royalists were sent in droves to the guillotine.

Over the next two and a half centuries, the owners of the house built on Crafford's property would include four New England families. This house is a monument not only to division caused by war, but also to reconciliation.

Old houses are more than the stone, wood, glass, and shingles from which they were built. If we listen hard enough, old houses remind us of the people who lived in them, and of their times.

www.ingramcontent.com/pod-product-compliance
Lightning Source LLC
Chambersburg PA
CBHW061730070526
44583CB00024B/3086